PIONEERS IN HISTORY

# REVOLUTIONARY POWER

## MICHAEL POLLARD

HEINEMANN

HEINEMANN CHILDREN'S REFERENCE
a division of Heinemann Educational Books Ltd
Halley Court, Jordan Hill, Oxford OX2 8EJ

OXFORD LONDON EDINBURGH
MELBOURNE SYDNEY AUCKLAND
MADRID ATHENS BOLOGNA
SINGAPORE IBADAN NAIROBI HARARE
GABORONE KINGSTON PORTSMOUTH NH(USA)

ISBN 0 431 00552 4

British Library Cataloguing in Publication Data
Pollard, Michael, 1931–
    Revolutionary power.
    1. Revolutions, history
    I. Title    II. Series
904'.7

© Heinemann Educational Books Ltd 1991
First published 1991

Designed by Pardoe Blacker Limited
Picture research by Faith Perkins
Maps by Kevin Diaper

Printed in Hong Kong

91 92 93 94 95 10 9 8 7 6 5 4 3 2 1

# Photographic credits

*a = above b = below r = right l = left*

The author and publishers wish to acknowledge, with
thanks, the following photographic sources:

The cover pictures are courtesy of The Bridgeman Art
Library and Peter Newark's Historical Pictures

J Allan Cash p7; Alexander Turnbull Library, Australia
p21*a*; Bridgeman Art Library pp5*b*, 9*b* (Trustees of the
Royal Society of Painters in Watercolour), 11*a* (Townley Art
Gallery and Museums, Burnley), 11*b*, 13*b*; Bulloz pp 14,
15*a*; Camera Press pp29, 33*a*, 37*b*, 38, 40, 41; Mary Evans
Picture Library pp21*b*, 23*a*; President of Ireland p26;
National Museum of Ireland p27; Billie Love Collection
p23*b*; Mansell Collection pp6, 16, 25*a*; Magnum pp31 (Cartier
Bresson), 35*b* (Bruno Barbey), 39 (Birt Glinn), 43*a* (James
Machtwey), 43*b* (Susan Meiselas); Peter Newark's
Historical Pictures pp5*a*, 9*a*, 15*b*, 28, 33*b*; Peter Newark's
Western Americana pp4, 10, 13*a*; Picturepoint pp17, 25*b*,
30, 35*a*; Popperfoto p37*a*; Scala pp 19*a* and *b*.

The publishers have made every effort to trace the copyright
holders, but if they have inadvertently overlooked any,
they will be pleased to make the necessary arrangements at
the first opportunity.

**Note to the reader**
In this book there are some words in the text which are printed in **bold** type. This shows that the word is
listed in the glossary on page 46. The glossary gives a brief explanation of words which may be new to you.

# Contents

# Introduction

Most people want to be ruled fairly, with fair laws and a fair share of their country's wealth. These things usually depend on the way a country is ruled by its **government**.

In many countries, there are at least two or three **political parties**, and people have the right to vote in **elections** for the party they think will speak and act for them. The party that wins the most votes forms the government. This type of government is called a **democracy**.

### Changing governments

In a democracy, elections are held every few years. If people dislike their government's actions, or **policies**, they can vote for a new government.

If a country is not a democracy, it is very difficult for people to change things. Sometimes they have to change the whole way the government works, and this is called a **revolution**.

Just as there are different types of government, there are different types of revolutions. Some only change the government, but others bring changes to people's whole way of life. In North America during the 1770s, for instance, a revolution put an American government in power instead of a British government far away in London. However, the Americans' way of life changed little. On the other hand, life in Russia after the 1917 revolution changed completely, with land being shared out among everyone instead of being owned by just a few.

◀ On 4 July 1776, during the American War of Independence, representatives from 13 territories in North America issued a Declaration of Independence. The declaration announced that the people living in the 13 territories no longer wished to be ruled by Britain.

Sometimes revolutions happen peacefully, but usually people have to fight for their freedom and many lives are lost. Some revolutions happen quickly, and others take years.

The revolution in Egypt in 1952 was over in a few weeks, for example, but the South Americans fought for nearly 20 years before they won their freedom from Spain in 1824. Even after a revolution, life under the new government may be worse than under the old. Revolutions bring change, but they can make life better or worse.

◀ On 14 July 1789, the Bastille, a prison in Paris, was attacked by French revolutionaries. This attack began the French Revolution, which completely changed the way France was ruled.

▼ The Russian Revolution of 1917 began with protests in the streets against shortages of food and coal. A few months later, the revolutionaries succeeded in ending the rule of the Russian monarchy.

# Boudicca, Queen of the Iceni

Today Britain is one country **ruled** by one queen. However, 2000 years ago several **Celtic** tribes lived in Britannia, as it was called, each with its own ruler.

Europe at the time was mostly ruled by the Romans. Then in AD43 they crossed the English Channel and soon **conquered** much of southern and central Britain. Some of the Celtic tribes welcomed the invading Romans, others did not.

The Iceni tribe lived in what is now East Anglia. Their king, Prasutagus, made a peace agreement, or **treaty**, with the Romans, who allowed him to go on ruling the Iceni. After Prasutagus died in AD60, the Romans broke the treaty and tried to take the Iceni lands. When Prasutagus' widow, Queen Boudicca, protested she was whipped by the Romans.

▲ Queen Boudicca rallying her people before the battle.

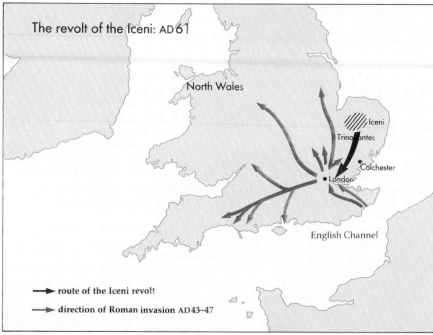

The revolt of the Iceni: AD61

North Wales

Iceni

Trinovantes

Colchester

London

English Channel

→ route of the Iceni revolt

→ direction of Roman invasion AD43–47

► Queen Boudicca riding in her war chariot. This statue was made in 1902 and the sculptor has added details which make the statue more dramatic. For example, today archaeologists know that there were no long knives attached to the wheels.

Boudicca was furious and led the Iceni into battle. They were joined by another tribe, the Trinovantes, who were angry because the Romans had made them pay heavy **taxes** in money and goods.

Boudicca first attacked the Roman town of Colchester and burned it to the ground. Most of the Roman army was on the other side of the country, fighting the people of North Wales. When news of Boudicca's **rebellion** reached the commander of the Roman army, he set out for London with his mounted soldiers, or **cavalry**. He left his foot soldiers to follow as quickly as they could.

As soon as the Roman commander reached London he realized that his foot soldiers would not arrive in time to protect the city, so he ordered the people to leave. Even so, there were still several thousand left when Boudicca attacked. Her army did not take prisoners and many people were killed, not only Romans but also the people who had been friendly with the invaders.

## The final battle

More and more people were joining Boudicca. Her army was now about eight times as strong as the Roman army. It was a threatening time for the Romans. If they did not stop the rebellion they might be driven out of Britain.

The two armies met somewhere north of London for the final battle. The Romans gathered at the top of a narrow valley and waited for Boudicca's army to charge. When the Celts reached them, the Romans hurled their spears. At the same time, the cavalry rode around the back of the Celts. Boudicca's army was trapped and thousands of her soldiers were killed by the Romans.

Boudicca managed to escape, but she knew her rebellion was over. She poisoned herself so that she would not be captured alive. The Romans had won and they were to rule Britain for nearly 400 years after their victory over Boudicca's army.

# Jeanne d'Arc

For over a hundred years, between 1337 and 1453, England and France were at war. The kings of England claimed that they also had a right to be the kings of France, and many battles were fought between the two countries. By the early 1400s, the English had won several victories, and by 1415 they controlled most of France.

Jeanne d'Arc was born in 1412, in the village of Domrémy in north-eastern France. When she was 13 she began hearing voices speaking to her in her parents' garden. Jeanne thought the voices were those of God and the saints. She believed they were telling her to save France from the English and to make sure that the French prince, the **Dauphin** Charles, was crowned king.

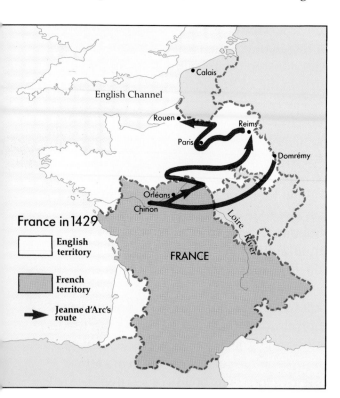

France in 1429

☐ English territory

▨ French territory

➤ Jeanne d'Arc's route

## The battle of Orléans

In 1428, when Jeanne was 17, the English surrounded the city of Orléans. By now the story of Jeanne's voices had spread, she was given help by the local army commander to travel south to Chinon, where the Dauphin was living.

The long journey took 11 days and Jeanne arrived in Chinon on 23 February 1429. At first the Dauphin did not believe Jeanne's story, but in April he agreed to allow her to go with his army to attack the English. Within two weeks the French, led by Jeanne, had freed Orléans.

For hundreds of years, the French kings had been crowned in the city of Reims. Jeanne's voices told her that her next task was to fight her way there with the Dauphin. The French army reached the city in July and Charles VII was crowned on 17 July, with Jeanne standing beside him.

## Saint or witch?

Stories of Jeanne's victories spread quickly and many French people came to believe that she was indeed a saint guided by the voice of God. Jeanne continued to fight the English, but in May 1430 she was taken prisoner by them. The leaders of the English army thought that Jeanne was a witch, not a saint, and they put her on trial. Charles VII, the man she had helped to become king of France, did nothing to help her. The English found Jeanne guilty and she was burned to death in Rouen on 30 May 1431.

▲ The meeting between Jeanne d'Arc and the Dauphin Charles at Chinon. When he agreed to let Jeanne march with his army to Orléans, Charles gave Jeanne a suit of white armour, a sword and a banner.

▶ On 8 May 1429, Jeanne rode at the head of the French soldiers as they paraded through the streets of Orléans. They had freed the city from the English in just 10 days and the people of Orléans now hold a festival every year, on 8 May, in memory of Jeanne's victory.

In the years following Jeanne's death, the French victories against the English continued. By 1453, the port of Calais was the only part of France still under English rule. The French people did not forget Jeanne d'Arc and many statues were built throughout France in her memory. In 1920, nearly 500 years after her death, Jeanne was recognized as a saint by the Pope, the leader of the Roman Catholic Church.

# The English Civil War

The beginning of the 1600s saw an argument between the King of England and his **Parliament**. This led to **civil war** between the supporters of each side. Today the British Parliament is the place where laws are made and where Members of Parliament, or MPs, vote on government policies. Although the Queen still has the right to refuse the laws that Parliament wants to make, no king or queen has done this for over 200 years.

▼ The Battle of Naseby took place on 14 June 1645. It was a crucial battle of the English Civil War because it ended with the defeat of the king. Oliver Cromwell was the leader of the army of Parliamentarian soldiers who defeated Charles I's forces at Naseby.

## King and Parliament

When Charles I came to the throne in 1625, things were very different. Like other kings at that time, Charles believed that he was chosen by God to rule and that he could do no wrong. Parliament had little power and Charles thought and said that it was a nuisance.

One of the few policies that Parliament could decide at that time was how much money people should pay in taxes. Charles needed money to rule, and the MPs hoped they could use their power to bargain with the King for more control in governing the country. Charles did not want this to happen and in 1629 he ordered Parliament to stop meeting.

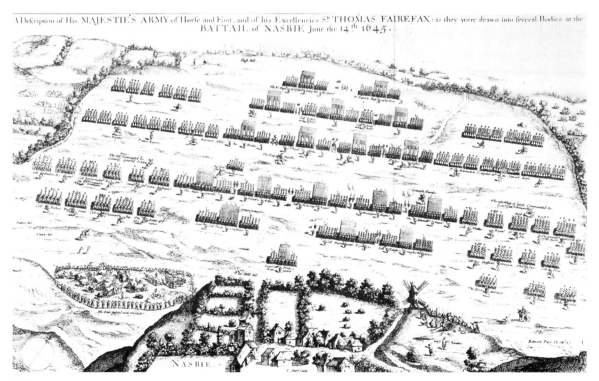

A Description of His MAJESTIE'S ARMY of Horse and Foot, and of his Excellencies S.r THOMAS FAIREFAX: as they were drawn into several Bodies at the BATTAIL of NASBIE June the 14.th 1645.

Ten years later war broke out with the Scots, and in 1640 Charles had to call Parliament because he needed money to pay his army. Parliament had not met for 11 years but when it did, the arguments between the King and Parliament began again.

In November 1641, the MPs drew up a list of things that they thought the King was doing wrong. It was called the Grand Remonstrance and it was passed through Parliament by just 11 votes. Then the MPs tried to take control of the army away from the King. Charles was furious and he led 400 soldiers to Parliament to arrest the leading MPs. A war between the supporters of Parliament, the Parliamentarians, and the Royalists who supported the King looked certain to happen.

---

### War breaks out

---

The first war between the Royalists and the Parliamentarians began in the summer of 1642 and lasted for nearly four years. The war was a time of great bitterness for the English, and even families were divided, brother against sister, mother against son, in their support for Royalists or Parliamentarians. Peace talks were held, but Charles refused to give up any of his power and he was imprisoned.

Charles managed to escape and the second war broke out during the summer of 1648. Late in the year, Charles I was captured and put on trial. He was **executed**, or put to death, in January 1649. Parliament had won the civil war and the balance of power in government. No king or queen of England was ever to have the same control in governing the country again.

▲ Oliver Cromwell at the head of the Parliamentarian army after his victory at the Battle of Marston Moor in 1644. After the death of Charles I, Cromwell ruled England until he died in 1658.

▼ Charles I was beheaded on 30 January 1649. It was a bitterly cold morning and he wore two shirts so that he would not shiver and appear frightened.

# American Independence

In 1607, three ships carrying about 100 English **settlers** sailed into what is today Chesapeake Bay, in the North American State of Maryland. These settlers built the first of 13 English **colonies** which they founded along the east coast of North America during the next 130 years. The settlements are called colonies because, although they were in America, they were ruled by the Parliament in London.

By the 1750s, the colonies had become important to Britain as suppliers of goods like cotton, timber and tobacco. Some of the timber was made into products such as tools and then sold back to the Americans. The British government tried to stop the colonists making these products more cheaply in America or from buying goods from other countries. The colonists also had to pay taxes to the government in London, although there was no one to speak for them in Parliament. The American colonists had their own way of life and they wanted to be free to govern themselves. They wanted to be **independent**.

## The first shots

The colonists' revolution started in a small way and built up slowly. In Boston in 1770, British troops killed five American colonists after a crowd threatened the soldiers with stones. Three years later, when the British government tried to make the Americans pay a tax on tea, a group of young Americans boarded British ships in Boston harbour and threw their cargo of tea into the water. This event became known as the Boston Tea Party.

The British responded by closing Boston harbour to shipping. The Americans then set up their own army of part-time soldiers. They were called 'minute men' because they were ready to fight at any minute.

1 New Hampshire
2 New York
3 Massachusetts Bay
4 Connecticut
5 Rhode Island
6 Pennsylvania
7 New Jersey
8 Maryland
9 Delaware
10 Virginia
11 North Carolina
12 South Carolina
13 Georgia

X site of battle

NORTH AMERICA

◄ The 13 colonies of North America which declared their independence from Britain in 1776.

The minute men kept their guns in a store at Concord, near Boston. In April 1775, the British sent soldiers to capture the guns, but the Americans were waiting for them at Lexington, halfway between Boston and Concord. Shots were fired and eight minute men were killed. The American War of Independence had begun.

▲ The Boston Tea Party took place on 16 December 1773. In response to the American protest, the British government passed the Boston Port Bill. The Bill meant that the port of Boston was closed until the American protesters had paid for the tea they had thrown into the harbour.

▶ General Cornwallis, the commander of the British forces, surrendered to George Washington at Yorktown on 19 October 1781. Here the red-coated British soldiers are marching out of their defences before laying down their guns in defeat.

## Fighting for freedom

The war went on for eight years. During this time, on 4 July 1776, the leaders of the colonies signed the Declaration of Independence, which said that the colonies were now independent States and no longer under the rule of the British. Then in 1781, the Americans won an important victory at Yorktown in Virginia. The war was nearly over, and a peace treaty was signed in September 1783. The Americans won the war, and just over five years later George Washington, who had commanded their forces, became the first **president** of the new United States of America.

# The French Revolution

The American War of Independence was watched with great interest in other parts of the world, and especially in France. Many French people thought change was needed in the government of their country as well. The King of France, Louis XVI, seemed to be less interested in governing France than in enjoying himself at his palace of Versailles, outside the capital, Paris. The King's way of life cost a lot of money. The French **peasants** who farmed the land paid money in taxes towards these expenses, but the nobles and other powerful people did not pay taxes at all.

Louis wanted to change the law to take away some of these special rights and to raise more money through taxes. The nobles, of course, did not want him to do this. At the same time, other French people wanted changes to give them more power and more control in government.

By the summer of 1789, violent protests, or **riots**, were taking place in the French countryside because many people were starving. There was little grain to make bread after a bad harvest the year before, and bread was very expensive. Some people met to set up an independent government. They wanted to make changes in the law to improve matters and end the riots. They stopped meeting when Louis told them to, but in Paris a rumour spread that they had been forced to do this by the King's own soldiers. This led to a riot in the city, when a mob destroyed a prison called the Bastille. The French Revolution had begun.

◀ The storming of the Bastille on 14 July 1789 was one of the first acts of the French Revolution. The Kings's own prisoners were kept in this castle, but when the Paris mob captured it, they found only seven people being held there. The mob then turned on the prison staff and killed them.

More riots followed throughout France, and in October 7000 people marched 20 kilometres from Paris to Versailles to demand bread. Louis promised to give them bread, but it was too late and he and the royal family were arrested.

## The rule of fear

During the French Revolution there were two kinds of people trying to change the way their country was governed. The **moderates** wanted to move forward slowly, but the **radicals** did not want to wait for gradual change. By the end of 1792, the radicals had taken over and they began to kill all the people they called 'enemies of the revolution'. The king and the royal family, and thousands of nobles, priests and other people were executed. No one felt safe during this two-year period, which became known as the Reign of Terror.

After 1794, life in France became calmer, but it was not until 1799 that the way the country was governed began to improve. This was the year the leader of the French army, Napoleon Bonaparte, took control of the government.

▲ Louis and his family were forced to live in Paris after the palace at Versailles was attacked. In June 1791 they escaped to Varennes, about 30 kilometres from Paris, but were arrested and brought back as prisoners.

▼ Louis XVI was beheaded by guillotine on 21 January 1793. Nine months later, Queen Marie Antoinette died in the same way. The Reign of Terror was a time when no one in France felt safe.

# Simón Bolívar

By the beginning of the 1800s, some European countries ruled other parts of the world. When one government rules other countries as well as its own, these countries are called its **empire**.

By 1800, South America was divided between the Spanish and the Portuguese empires. Like the North American colonists before them, many South Americans wanted independence from foreign rule and to set up their own governments. In 1808, the French invaded Spain and put a Frenchman on the Spanish throne instead of King Ferdinand VII. The colonists of South America took this opportunity to begin their revolution, hoping that the Spaniards would be weakened by their troubles at home.

▶ The Spanish and Portuguese colonies in South America in 1800. In 1830, after the union broke up, Quito was renamed Ecuador. New Granada later become Colombia.

▲ Simón Bolívar was born in the Spanish colony of Venezuela in 1783, the son of a Spanish noble. As a young man he travelled widely in Europe and became interested in the ideas of the French Revolution.

Jamaica

•Caracas

Atlantic Ocean

Venezuela

Battle
of Boyacá
1819

New Granada

Quito

Amazon River

SOUTH
AMERICA

Spanish territory

Portuguese territory

Pacific Ocean

Andes Mountains

Rio de
Janeiro•

Buenos
Aries•

There were two freedom armies in South America, one in the south and one in the north. The northern revolution was led by a man called Simón Bolívar.

At first Bolívar and his army had many successes, and he became known as The Liberator, or the person who brings freedom. However, in 1814 Ferdinand VII returned to the Spanish throne, determined to crush the revolution. More and more Spanish soldiers were sent to South America. The revolution failed and in 1815 Bolívar chose to leave South America and live in **exile** in Jamaica.

## The freedom march

Bolívar returned to South America in 1816, landing with a small army in Venezuela. Two years later he had freed part of Venezuela and was planning to attack the Spaniards in New Granada, which is in the north-west corner of South America. To reach New Granada, Bolívar and his soldiers had to wade through 200 kilometres of swamps and cross ten rivers. They were always wet and clouds of mosquitoes made life even more miserable. Then they had to cross the high Andes Mountains, where many of the soldiers and all their horses died in the icy cold. The journey took three exhausting months.

On 7 August 1819, Bolívar's army defeated the Spaniards at the battle of Boyacá, freeing New Granada from its Spanish rulers. This was not the last battle of the revolution, but it was the most important. Later that year, Bolívar announced the **union** of the independent states of Venezuela, New Granada and Quito.

▲ A monument to Simón Bolívar in Caracas, the capital city of Venezuela. In South America, Bolívar is also known as 'the Liberator' in honour of his freeing the region from Spanish rule.

## The end of a dream

The war of independence came to an end in 1824, and South America was at last free of Spanish rule. Bolívar's dream was that South American states should **unite**, as those in North America had done. This dream was never to become a reality. There were wars between some of the South American states, and civil war in others. In 1830, the union broke up and Venezuela, New Granada and Quito separated. Bolívar died in the same year, a disappointed man.

# Garibaldi and the Red Shirts

Italy today is one country, but just over 150 years ago it was made up of many separate states, some of which had foreign rulers. Many Italians wanted their lands to be joined into one country, with one government. A group called Young Italy was formed to work for unity and independence.

In 1833, a young sailor, Giuseppe Garibaldi, joined Young Italy. The group was **plotting** against the King of Piedmont, and Garibaldi's job was to persuade the navy to join them. When their plot failed,

The union of Italy 1859 to 1870

FRANCE
SWITZERLAND
AUSTRIAN EMPIRE
Savoy 1860
Lombardy 1859
Venetia 1866
→ Garibaldi's route
Piedmont
Parma 1860
Nice 1860
Modena 1860
Tuscany 1860
Corsica
Papal States 1860
Rome
Naples
Sardinia
Kingdom of the Two Sicilies 1860 (1871)
Mediterranean Sea
Palermo

▲ In 1830, the country we now call Italy was made up of separate states, many of which had foreign rulers. Lombardy and Venetia were ruled by Austria, Naples and Sicily were ruled by a Spaniard, and Modena, Parma and Tuscany were ruled by Austrian dukes.

many members of Young Italy had to leave Europe to escape being captured and shot. Garibaldi fled to South America, where he lived in exile for 14 years, taking part in local revolutions.

## Garibaldi's return

In 1848, revolutions broke out in a number of European countries, including Italy. Garibaldi hurried home, bringing with him about 60 friends who had fought alongside him in South America. They had no proper uniforms, but they all wore the same coloured shirts and this gave them their name, the Red Shirts.

The revolution of 1848 to 1849 did not bring freedom and unity to the Italian states, because Garibaldi and his followers had to fight against larger armies who had better weapons. However, it did give the Red Shirts a useful training in warfare. They found that quick surprise attacks against the enemy were very successful. This type of fighting is called **guerrilla warfare**.

## One country, one king

In 1849, Garibaldi had to escape into exile once again. He returned to Italy in 1854 and five years later he helped to train a guerrilla army which fought in northern Italy, driving the foreign rulers out of some areas. At the same time, revolutions were successful in central Italy, and afterwards the King of Sardinia, Victor Emanuel II, was asked to rule the freed areas.

▶ In 1860, hundreds of mainland Italians joined Garibaldi to fight on the island of Sicily and this army became known as the Thousand. With Sicilian help, Garibaldi's 1000 Red Shirts drove the King of Naples' army of 20000 soldiers off the island.

Then, in 1860, the people of the island of Sicily asked Garibaldi to help them organize a revolution against their ruler, the King of Naples. The war in Sicily was an enormous victory for the Red Shirts, who chased the King of Naples' army out of Sicily and back to the mainland. Garibaldi's followers went on to capture Naples, which in 1861 joined the other areas under Victor Emmanuel's rule.

The fight for a united Italy continued for another nine years. By 1870 the battle was over and Italy was one country, with Victor Emmanuel II as its first king.

▶ Garibaldi believed passionately in the idea of a united Italy and his powerful personality encouraged others to fight for the same cause. Garibaldi died in 1882, 12 years after his dream of one country under one government came true.

# The New Zealand Land Wars

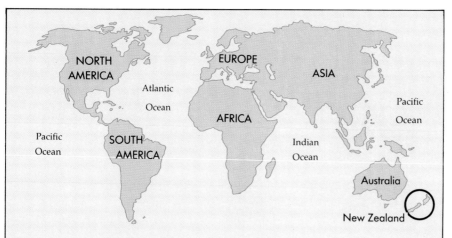

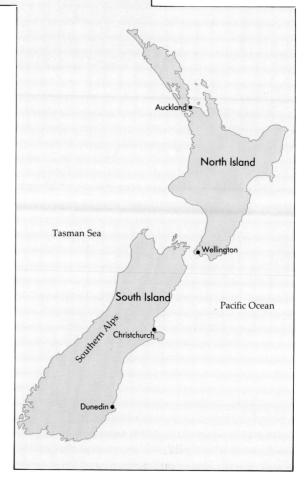

▼ New Zealand is made up of a North and South Island with several smaller outlying islands. The country extends over 1750 kilometres from north to south.

The first people to settle in New Zealand were the Maoris, who travelled there by canoe from islands in the South Pacific Ocean over 1000 years ago. They were great warriors and often fought each other, usually over the ownership of land. For this reason, the Maoris often built a high wooden fence around a plot of land near their villages. They sheltered in these stockades in times of war.

The first European to sight New Zealand was the Dutch **explorer**, Abel Tasman. He sailed up the coast in 1642 and planned to land and explore, but Maoris in canoes fought his men off before they could reach the shore. The first Europeans to land there, in 1769, were sailors from Captain Cook's ship, the *Endeavour*. Some years later, the first settlers came to New Zealand.

In 1840, Britain took over New Zealand as part of its empire. The British government made a treaty with Maori leaders, allowing them to keep their lands. This promise was soon broken, however, and settlers bought land from people who did not really own it.

▲ The treaty of Waitangi was signed by the British and the Maoris on 6 February 1840. In the treaty Britain undertook to protect Maori rights and in return the Maoris accepted British rule.

## The fight for land

When the Maoris realised they had been cheated, they began attacking settlements to try to drive the British out of their country. Many men, women and children died, both Maori and British. There was peace for a while, but the settlers went on trying to trick the Maoris out of their lands. At last, in 1860, war broke out again between the Maoris and the British.

The British were surprised by the Maoris' skill in warfare. **Traders** who had come to New Zealand in the 1790s had sold the Maoris guns, with which they had become expert. They used their stockades as forts, and these were difficult for the British to capture. Most important of all, the Maoris were determined to win and they fought long and hard. The British had more soldiers and better guns, but it seemed they could not defeat the Maori warriors.

# The New Zealand Land Wars

## The long struggle

The war went on for five years. At last, with many of their people dead, the Maoris seemed to be beaten. The British did not want the expense of keeping a large army in New Zealand and they sent most of the soldiers home. Some Maoris had not given up hope of freeing their country, however, and there were more battles during the next seven years. By 1871, nearly all the Maoris had been defeated. Their revolution had failed and they could no longer stop their lands being sold to the British.

▼ The Maori Wars were caused by British settlers in New Zealand breaking the terms of the Treaty of Waitangi. During the wars many more Maoris than British settlers were killed, and large areas of Maori land were seized by British soldiers.

# The Boxer Rising

By the end of the 1800s, the people of China were worried about what the rest of the world was planning to do with their country. Foreign traders had been coming to China for a long time, hoping to make money. Then **missionaries** came, hoping to convert the Chinese to Christianity. The foreigners won wars about trade, and by the 1860s Britain, France and Russia had taken over parts of the Chinese empire. When Japan tried to take Korea in 1894, it led to a war which Japan won.

Some Chinese wanted to drive the foreigners out of the country. Others thought it was more important to stop the foreigners taking over the rest of the Chinese empire. They believed that there would have to be changes in China itself, before they were strong enough to do this.

For example, new farming methods had to be taught to produce better crops and make more money. The ruler of China, the Emperor Guang Xu, agreed and in 1898 he began putting these plans into action.

There had been few changes in China for thousands of years, however, and many people were against the Emperor Guang Xu's plans. Guang Xu's aunt, the Empress Ci Xi, was very powerful and she led the Chinese who were opposed to the changes. She had Guang Xu and his followers arrested.

## The Boxers

For a long time, there had been a secret Chinese group, whose members hated the foreigners. They practised a kind of boxing

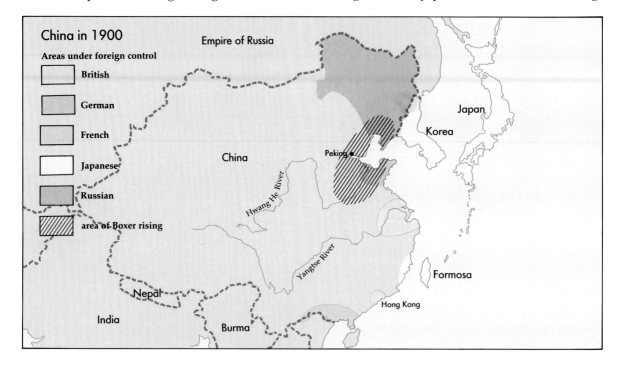

China in 1900

Areas under foreign control

- British
- German
- French
- Japanese
- Russian
- area of Boxer rising

Empire of Russia

Japan

Korea

China

Peking

Hwang He River

Yangtse River

Formosa

Hong Kong

Nepal

India

Burma

and they became known as the Boxers. By 1900, the Boxers had a huge following mainly due to the failure of the rice crop because of drought. The people were starving. The Boxers also had the support of the Empress Ci Xi, at first secretly, and later, openly.

In China, the foreigners lived mainly in settlements in the cities. The Boxers began attacking the foreign settlements, and many people were murdered. Chinese Christians were also killed, because Christianity was a foreign religion.

▲ During the Boxer Rising the rebels posted up notices which declared 'Death to the Foreigners'.

In 1900, a Boxer army surrounded Peking and on 21 June the Empress declared war against the foreigners. In the following weeks, more people died. Foreigners' homes, shops and factories were destroyed, and churches were burned.

In August an international army reached Peking and defeated the Boxers. The Empress Ci Xi had to sign a peace treaty agreeing to pay for the damage that had been done to property. Foreign soldiers stayed in Peking to protect the peace, and the Boxer leaders were executed.

Most revolutions aim to bring about change, but the Empress Ci Xi and the Boxers tried to keep things the same. Even so, a great change was coming. The people turned against the emperors and in 1911 China became a **republic** governed by a president.

▲ The emperor Guang Xu belonged to the Qing dynasty, whose emperors had ruled China since the end of the Ming dynasty in 1644. Guang Xu was the last emperor to rule China, which became a republic in 1911.

# Kemal Atatürk

During the 1800s, the extent of the once great Ottoman Empire was being reduced by her more powerful European neighbours.

The Ottoman ruler, the Sultan, also had to face problems within the empire itself, particularly in Turkey. During the late 1890s, revolutionary groups in Turkey were becoming more interested in the changes that were taking place in Europe. There, new inventions were improving life at work and new ideas were giving people more freedom to do and say what they liked. All over the world, revolutions had given people more control in the government of their countries.

## The army takes over

In Turkey in 1909, there was a revolution by army officers who put a new sultan on the throne and took the most important government jobs for themselves.

When the First World War broke out in 1914, the Turks sided with Germany against the **Allies**. The Turks chose the losing side and, after the war ended in 1918, France, Britain, Italy and Greece divided what remained of the Ottoman Empire between them. It seemed the Allies would even take Turkey, helped by the Sultan whom they had returned to power.

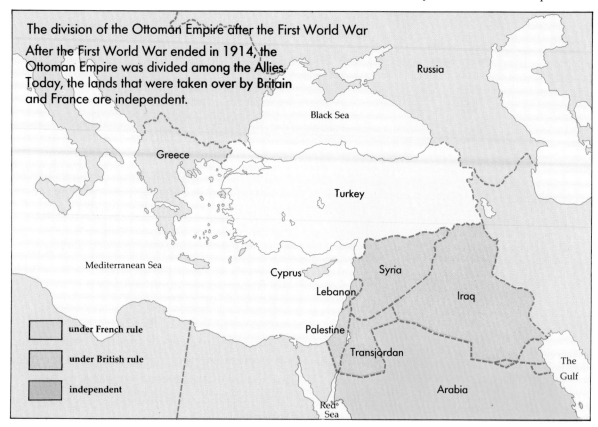

The division of the Ottoman Empire after the First World War

After the First World War ended in 1914, the Ottoman Empire was divided among the Allies. Today, the lands that were taken over by Britain and France are independent.

Russia

Black Sea

Greece

Turkey

Mediterranean Sea

Cyprus

Syria

Lebanon

Iraq

□ under French rule

Palestine

□ under British rule

Transjordan

The Gulf

□ independent

Arabia

Red Sea

► Mustafa Kemal was born in 1881. He won many battles against the Allies in the First World War, and became a national hero in Turkey.

▼ Under Kemal's rule many things changed in Turkey. He forbad men to wear turbans and fezzes. Women were allowed to vote. He insisted that the Roman alphabet was used in place of the Arabic one. This monument to Kemal stands in front of the university in Istanbul.

## Kemal's revolution

By 1918, Mustafa Kemal was the only Turkish general who remained unbeaten in battle. After the war, he became the leader of the **nationalists**, who believed that Turkey should stay united and independent. When the Greeks invaded Turkey in May 1919, Kemal led the fight to drive them out. His army succeeded in 1922 and the next year Turkey became a republic. The Sultan escaped on a British battleship and Kemal became Turkey's first elected president. In the 1930s, he took a new name, Kemal Atatürk, meaning 'Kemal, father of the Turks'.

Kemal remained president of Turkey until his death in 1938. He worked hard to make the changes that he and other Turks had admired in Europe. Some thought the changes came too quickly, but Atatürk had, and still has, many supporters who believe he really was 'the father of the Turks'.

# Fighting for Ireland

People have been looking for an answer to the 'Irish question' for hundreds of years. Should part of Ireland be governed by the British Parliament in London, or should all of Ireland be an independent country?

Most of Ireland has been independent since the 1920s, when the Irish Free State was set up in the south. Today that part of the country is called the Republic of Eire. The remaining part, the north-east, is still under British rule and is called Ulster.

## North against south

In 1913, it looked as though the British Parliament would give a form of independence to the whole of Ireland. They suggested Home Rule. Under Home Rule, there was to be a parliament in Dublin to manage home, or Irish, affairs, while other policies such as taxation would still be decided in London.

Many of the **Protestant** people of Ulster were against the idea of Home Rule. They distrusted the Catholic southerners and wanted to continue being governed by Britain. They formed a part-time army called the Ulster Volunteers to fight the supporters of Home Rule. The southerners set up the Irish Volunteers, which later became the Irish Republican Army, or IRA.

In 1914, the First World War broke out and the arguments died down for a while. Then, on Easter Monday 1916, a group of southerners declared an independent Irish republic. They belonged to the Sinn Fein party and their rebellion came to be called the Easter Uprising. The fighting lasted a week and afterwards the British government executed most of the leaders.

◄ During the Easter Uprising the streets of Dublin were turned into a battlefield. An army of 2000 members of Sinn Fein shot at British soldiers from behind barricades which they had built throughout the city. The British soldiers used cannons to put down the rebellion.

▲ Eamon de Valera was one of the leaders of the Easter Uprising. In 1919, Michael Collins helped him to escape from prison in England and de Valera was elected president of the republican government in Dublin. During the civil war in the south, de Valera fought against supporters of the Anglo-Irish treaty, including his old friend, Michael Collins.

Two years later, Sinn Fein MPs left the British Parliament and set up their own parliament, called the Dail, in Dublin. In January 1919, they again declared the whole of Ireland an independent republic. Nearly three years of war followed, with bitter fighting between the IRA and British soldiers, before the two countries signed the Ango-Irish Treaty setting up the Irish Free State. The British government withdrew its soldiers and recognized the independence of the Dail. Ulster was to

have its own parliament, and it chose to remain part of Britain.

The troubles were not yet over, though, and civil war broke out in the south between the supporters of the treaty and the people who did not want Ulster to be a separate country.

## The bitter harvest

The civil war in southern Ireland ended in 1923, and the supporters of the treaty won. Even so, many Irish people still want Ulster and Eire to be united. This has led to the violence that still continues today in Ulster. As yet, there is no answer to the Irish question.

▼ In the two Irelands, the fighting has been as much about religion as about union. Most of the Ulster Irish are Protestant, while the majority of people in Eire are Catholic. Ulster is the smaller country and union would bring a government with a Catholic majority. Most Ulster Protestants are against this.

The division of Ireland

# The Russian Revolution

Russia 1922

On 16 April 1917, a train pulled into the station in Petrograd, which was then Russia's capital city. A huge crowd cheered as a man with a short pointed beard climbed out. The man was called Lenin and he had come back to Russia after 12 years in exile.

Lenin was leader of a group called the Bolsheviks, and he had been sent into exile by the Russian king, Tsar Nicholas II, because of his political beliefs. The Bolsheviks thought that the government should be run by the workers and the peasants, and not by kings like the Tsar.

## The workers rise up

A few weeks before Lenin's return in 1917, there was a revolution in Petrograd. There were several reasons why the workers had

started the revolution. Since the beginning of the First World War in 1914, thousands of Russian soldiers had died, and the Russian people no longer believed that the Tsar could lead their armies to victory against the Germans. There were also food shortages and prices kept going up.

The revolution began with a **strike** by 200000 workers. When the Tsar ordered his troops to use force against the strikers, the soldiers refused. On 15 March, the

▲ Lenin died in 1924, but his revolutionary ideas continued to live on in the policies of the Communist Party. This Russian poster of 1940 declares 'We say LENIN by which we mean the PARTY. We say the PARTY by which we mean LENIN'.

Tsar gave up the throne, and the Russian Parliament then set up a provisional government. This is a government that looks after everyday needs until an elected government takes over.

## Lenin takes control

Lenin thought that the changes made by the provisional government did not go far enough. He wanted the nobles' land to be taken from them and given to the peasants, and he wanted Russia to stop fighting Germany. Early in November the Bolsheviks seized control of Petrograd. This was the beginning of a civil war in Russia which lasted for over two years. On one side there were the Bolsheviks, whose forces became known as the Red armies. On the other were the White armies, who opposed the Bolsheviks.

The battle between the two sides was long and bitter. The murder of the Tsar and his family in July 1918 was just one of the horrors of the war. All over Russia, millions starved or were killed in the fighting. At last, late in 1920, the Red armies won.

In many ways, the Russian people still had no more freedom than they had had under the Tsar. Although Lenin allowed elections to be held for the Parliament, for example, he stopped the parties who were against the Bolsheviks, or **Communists** as they were now known, from holding political meetings. After Lenin died in January 1924, the struggle for a better form of government in Russia went on.

▼ People queueing for food in Moscow in 1933. Food shortages were one of the main causes of the Russian Revolution, but they were a problem which a change of government did not cure.

# Gandhi and India

By 1947, the British government had ruled India for 90 years, but the British had lived there for much longer. Traders began to be interested in Indian spices and other goods in the early 1600s. Trading settlements were built by the British East India Company, and by the 1820s, the Company's officials and army controlled India. The British continued to profit from Indian goods into the next century. Indian cotton and tea were sold and most of the money went to the British people, who made even more money by weaving the cotton in factories in Britain and then selling it back to the Indians.

India is a huge country of many different people. There are also many religions, of which the largest groups are Hindus and Muslims. The British made many changes in India, building railways and canals, and introducing British education and laws. All this work was organized by the Indian Civil Service and paid for out of Indian taxes. The leading positions in the Civil Service were held by British people. Indians were trained to do office work, but they were not allowed to have important jobs. Many thought it was time for a change.

## A man of peace

Mohandas Gandhi was an Indian who trained as a lawyer in Britain. Later he took a job in South Africa and worked for the rights of Indians there. Gandhi was a Hindu, and after he returned to India in 1914 he joined the Congress party, which was largely made up of Hindus. The Muslims had their own party called the Muslim League.

◀ Mohandas Gandhi was born in 1869. He was a religious Hindu and he tried to live simply. When Gandhi returned to India in 1914, a poet gave him the name of Mahatma, which means 'great soul'. Soon this was the name by which he was known to millions. This monument to Gandhi is in New Delhi, in India.

By the end of 1916 both parties were calling for freedom from British rule, but independence took another 30 years. During this time some Indians, led by Gandhi, believed that India would win independence peacefully. Others disagreed with him and there were many riots, during which thousands of people were killed.

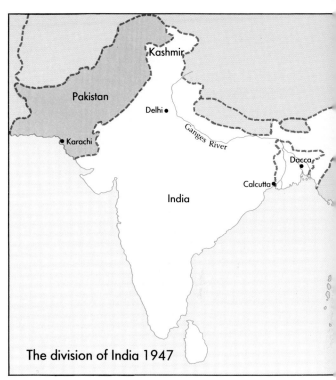

The division of India 1947

▲ The division of the old India after independence in 1947. In 1971, India supported a revolution in East Pakistan, which became the indpendent country of Bangladesh.

## Independence for India

India gained its freedom on 15 August 1947, but the troubles were not over. There had long been a struggle between the Muslim League and the Hindus' Congress party over who would govern the country. At independence, the old India was divided into two countries. Pakistan was to be for the Muslims, and India for the Hindus. Violence broke out as Pakistan's Hindus rushed to join their own people in India, and India's Muslims tried to reach Pakistan. A year after independence, Gandhi, the man of peace, was murdered by a Hindu gunman.

▲ Gandhi organized peaceful meetings and marches, but he was often put in prison by the British, who were worried about his power over the Indian people. This photograph of Gandhi was taken in 1948, during the last few months of his life.

# Mao Tse-tung

In 1911 there was a revolution in China and 2500 years of rule by emperors came to an end. China became a republic and its first president, Sun Yat-sen, promised democracy and a better way of life. Unfortunately, change did not happen as quickly as Sun Yat-sen hoped. Some people opposed his leadership and he had to resign later that year. He returned to power in 1917, but he was unable to govern successfully. When Sun Yat-sen died in 1925, a man called Chiang Kai-shek became president, but there was still little improvement to most people's way of life.

The Chinese were tired of promises. Many admired the new Russian government, and in 1921, a Chinese Communist Party was set up, like the one in Russia. The Communists believed that the peasants and workers should control their fields, their factories and their government. However, Chiang Kai-shek did not want Communism in China. In 1927, his soldiers began killing Chinese Communists.

## Escape to freedom

The Communist leaders who escaped, organized their own forces and began to fight back. Among them was Mao Tse-tung, who had been one of the founders of the Chinese Communist Party. Mao's Red Army set up its headquarters in the southern

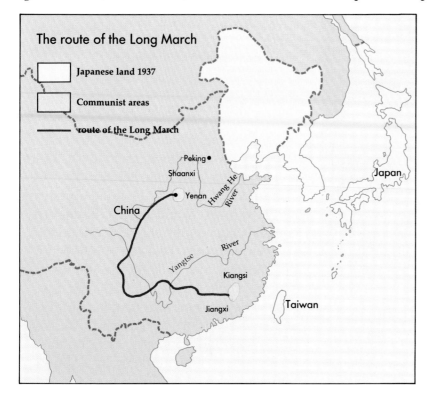

The route of the Long March

☐ Japanese land 1937

▨ Communist areas

— route of the Long March

Peking ●
Shaanxi
Yenan
China
Hwang He River
Japan
Yangtse River
Kiangsi
Jiangxi
Taiwan

◀ As Mao's Red Army was beginning its Long March from Jiangxi province, the armies of the other Communist leaders were also setting off from their bases throughout eastern China.

province of Jiangxi, but they were soon attacked by Chiang's troops. The Red Army lost many battles, and the Communists decided to escape to the north.

Mao and the Red Army set off in October 1934. Little did they know that they would have to travel nearly 10000 kilometres before their journey ended. During their Long March, as it became known, they fought many battles and suffered great hardships. When they reached the northern province of Shaanxi in October 1935, only 20000 remained of the 100000 or so people who had set out a year earlier.

▲ In 1966, Chairman Mao announced that there was to be a Cultural Revolution in China, to bring about political and social change throughout the country. Many young people, who became known as Red Guards, helped to carry out Mao's ideas, attacking anything that was thought to be foreign or old-fashioned. Mao's ideas were published in *The Little Red Book* which became a famous feature of the Cultural Revolution.

## The final victory

By 1935, Chiang Kai-shek had more to worry about than the Communists. The Japanese had **invaded** north-eastern China in 1931, and since then they had captured land to the south and the west. In 1937, the Communists kidnapped Chiang and forced him to sign a peace treaty, agreeing to fight the Japanese with them.

In 1939, the Second World War broke out. It ended in 1945, with the defeat of Japan. In July 1946 Chiang's troops attacked the Communists again. This time Mao's victory was final. In 1949, Chiang and followers fled to the island of Taiwan. On 1 October, Mao Tse-tung proclaimed the new People's Republic of China.

▲ Mao Tse-tung was born in 1893 and was a student when China became a republic in 1911. In 1921, he helped to set up the Chinese Communist Party and he became its chairman during the Long March of 1934 to 1935. Mao remained leader of the republic until his death in 1976.

# Gamal Abdel Nasser

In many countries, revolutions have been started by army or navy officers. One of these countries is Egypt, where the Free Officers' Revolution took place in 1952. The king, Farouk, had to leave the country and Egypt became a republic in 1953.

The Egyptian revolution was not just to remove King Farouk, however. Ever since the British took over Egypt from the Ottoman sultan in 1882, the British had played a part in the way Egypt was governed. Even when Egypt was given its independence in 1922, British soldiers remained in the country and their presence angered the Egyptians.

One of the main reasons for Britain's interest in Egypt was the Suez Canal. The canal is an important route for ships travelling between the Mediterranean Sea and the Indian Ocean. Even after the

Second World War ended in 1945, British soldiers were still stationed in the area called the Canal Zone.

## War and revolution

In 1948, the Jewish State of Israel was declared in Palestine, a country that had belonged to the Arabs. This greatly angered Egypt and other Arab countries. They began a war with Israel, but they were quickly defeated. The Egyptians blamed King Farouk and his government for Egypt's weakness both in war and in the country's failure to free itself from the British. In 1951, the Egyptians attacked British bases in the Canal Zone, and British-owned buildings were set on fire in the capital, Cairo. The Free Officers' Revolution took place within the year.

▶ The Suez Canal is important to trade even today, because it is a much quicker route between the Mediterranean Sea and the Indian Ocean than sailing around Africa. During the Suez Crisis of 1956, the Egyptians stopped foreign ships using the canal. It was opened again in 1957, and Egypt was able to collect the money paid by ships to pass through it.

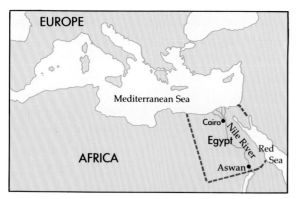

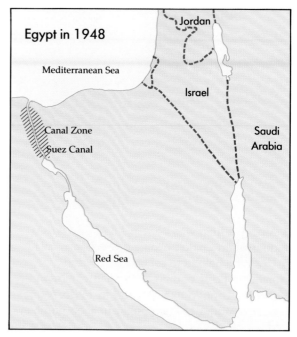

► Since its opening in 1869, the Suez Canal has been deepened to take the much larger ships which now travel along it.

▼ Gamal Abdel Nasser was born in 1918, the son of a post office worker and the first of 11 children. He was to become the first native-born ruler of an independent Egypt in over 2000 years. By the mid-1950s, he had also become the leader of a movement for unity among the Arab countries of the Middle East.

### Friend of the people

The leader of the Free Officers was an army colonel, Gamal Abdel Nasser. He became leader of the country in 1954, and in the same year Britain agreed to remove its soldiers by June 1956.

Egypt is a large country, but most of it is desert which makes it very difficult to earn a living from farming. One of Nasser's ideas was to build the Aswan High Dam on the Nile River. Water from the dam was used to irrigate the desert, to make more land suitable for farming. Nasser also built schools and hospitals for the people, as well as factories to provide more jobs. Water from the Aswan High Dam was used to make electricity to power the new factories.

Before he could build the dam, Nasser had to raise enough money. To do this, he decided to take over the Suez Canal, which was owned by a British and French company. In 1956, Britain and France made a secret agreement with Israel to capture the canal and overthrow Nasser. The attack failed. Instead of destroying Nasser, it made Egyptians and other Arabs admire him more than ever. He was still a popular leader when he died in 1970.

# *Jomo Kenyatta*

By 1900, most of the huge continent of Africa was ruled by six European countries. The foreigners first came as traders, then settlers arrived to farm Africa's fertile land and to mine its gold and diamonds.

British settlers started to arrive in Kenya about 1900. By 1915, nearly two million hectares of land had been taken from two farming peoples, the Masai and the Kikuyu. The settlers called their land the White Highlands and it was for Europeans only. The Masai and Kikuyu were put in special areas, called **reserves**, where the land was too poor to support them. By 1948, there were 30 000 white settlers in Kenya, and five million black Kenyans who had no say in how their country was governed.

Two things changed all this. One was the return of black Kenyans who had fought for Britain in the Second World War, and who had seen the freedom of people in other countries. The other was the return of one man, Jomo Kenyatta, who had left Kenya, to travel to England, 17 years before.

## The Mau Mau

Jomo Kenyatta was a member of the Kikuyu tribe, and he had gone to London in 1929 to study law. Independence groups had been set up in the 1920s in Kenya, but a strong leader was needed to unite the different tribes.

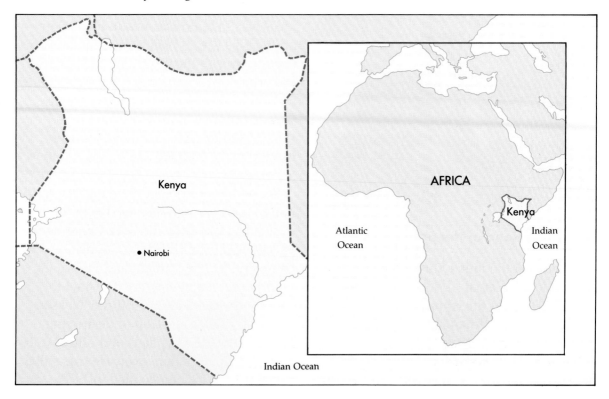

The white settlers in Kenya wanted to stay British and would not even talk about independence. Then, in 1952, members of a Kikuyu secret society called the Mau Mau began attacking white settlers and black Kenyans who supported British rule. Farms were burned and some people were killed. The British sent in troops, and soon the Mau Mau was fighting a guerrilla war against an army which was larger and better equipped. In three years, about 30 settlers died, but thousands of Kikuyu were killed. Although Kenyatta said that he had nothing to do with the Mau Mau, he was put in prison in December 1952.

▲ After the Mau Mau attacks began in 1952, thousands of black Kenyans were held under guard in detention camps because the British thought they might be members of the Mau Mau.

## An independent Africa

When Kenyatta was released in 1961, many African countries were already free of foreign rule. The British government was planning independence for Kenya, but there were problems getting the different tribes to agree on the new type of government.

Kenyatta was a man of great charm and a powerful leader, and he was able to guide Kenya to independence in 1963. The white settlers were allowed to stay on, and Kenyatta was able to persuade all Kenyans to work together. By the time he died in 1978, he had made Kenya into one of Africa's most peaceful independent countries.

▲ Jomo Kenyatta became the first prime minister of independent Kenya in 1963. After the country became a republic a year later, he became president and held the position until his death in 1978.

# Fidel Castro

For 400 years the Caribbean island of Cuba was a Spanish colony. The United States helped the Cubans to drive the Spaniards out in the 1890s, but afterwards the American army governed the island. Although Cuba was independent, many Cubans thought their country was still too closely linked to the United States. Cuba's main crop is sugar, and by that time most of the sugar plantations were owned by American companies.

The Cubans were also unhappy with their government. Their leaders seemed to be concerned only with power and money. In 1934, one of these **corrupt** politicians, Fulgencio Batista, seized control of the government. This type of government, when someone rules who has not been elected, is called a **dictatorship**. Batista won an election in 1940, but lost in 1944. Eight years later he overthrew the government and again became a dictator.

This time a lawyer called Fidel Castro was one of the first to oppose Batista. In July 1953, he led an unsuccessful attack on an army camp, and a few days later he was put in prison. After his release in 1955, Castro decided to leave Cuba for Mexico, where he and his followers trained in guerrilla warfare. A year later, they returned to Cuba secretly and their war against Batista began. Gradually support for Castro grew, and more and more Cubans joined his army. On 1 January 1959, Batista fled the country, and a few weeks later Castro became head of the Cuban government.

◄ Fidel Castro inspects a farming project, part of the plan he began after becoming Cuban leader to improve the Cuban people's way of life. Roads, hospitals and schools were built in country areas, and in 1961, the Year of Education, 120 000 teachers were sent throughout Cuba to teach reading and writing to the people.

The missile crisis

▲ Cuba is only about 200 kilometres from the southern tip of the United States. During the early 1960s, the United States government was worried that their country would be attacked by the Soviet Union's missiles based in Cuba.

## Cuba and the United States

Castro quickly took back Cuban land from the American companies. When he refused to pay for it, the United States stopped buying Cuban sugar. The American government then became worried about the friendship between Cuba and the Soviet Union, who had agreed to buy the sugar instead.

The United States helped to plan an invasion of Cuba by Cubans who had fled from Castro. This landing, at the Bay of Pigs, failed, but in October 1962 American spy planes discovered Soviet missiles in Cuba. For a week it looked as though there would be a nuclear war between the United States and the Soviet Union. Fortunately, both sides came to an agreement.

## Friends and enemies

Castro has done much to improve life in Cuba, but his actions continue to divide the way people think about him. He is a hero in countries like Mozambique in Africa, where he sent Cuban soldiers to join in a revolution. On the other hand, in non-Communist countries like the United States, many people still distrust Castro because of his friendship with the Soviet Union.

▼ In April 1989, the Soviet leader, President Gorbachev, visited Cuba for talks with President Castro.

# Ayatollah Khomeini

The followers of the Islamic religion are called Muslims, and although there are different Muslim groups, the two largest are Sunnites and Shi'ites. The Shi'ites are very strict Muslims who believe that every word of the holy book of Mohammed, the Koran, must be obeyed. In Iran, most people are Shi'ites.

Until 1979, Iran was ruled by a king, the Shah, but although Iran is an oil-rich country, only a few people enjoyed its wealth. The Shah used his power to help himself and his family, but he also tried to improve his people's way of life. Many of his plans failed, however, and his efforts to change farming were not successful. By the 1970s, much of Iran's food had to be imported and in the countryside many people were starving. Both the Shah and his father before him had introduced ideas from Europe and the United States, such as education and jobs for women. The more religious Shi'ites thought these changes were wrong.

▼ Mohammed Reza Pahlavi became Shah of Iran in 1941, during the Second World War. In 1979, violent protests against the Shah's rule drove him into exile and he died the following year.

## The last days of the Shah

In 1953, the Shah was forced into exile by a revolution. Helped by the United States, the army defeated the revolutionaries and the Shah soon returned. Afterwards, he began building up the navy, army and air force to protect his throne and to make Iran the most powerful country in the Middle East. He also set up a secret police force, SAVAK, to destroy his enemies in Iran.

By the late 1970s, even SAVAK could not quieten the Shah's enemies. Some people wanted Iran to become a republic, but the religious groups wanted far greater changes and they had the largest following. In 1978, there were protest meetings in the universities and riots in the towns, including the capital, Tehran. The Shah tried to use the army to bring order, but the protests grew. In January 1979, he left Iran with his family, on what was described as a holiday. He never returned.

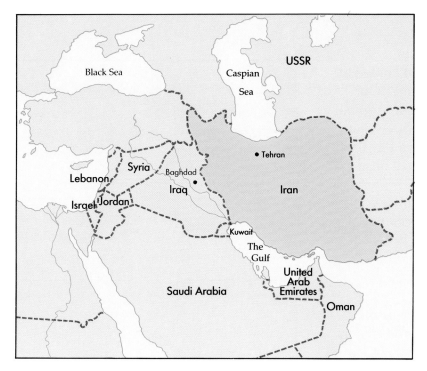

▼ Ayatollah Khomeini was nearly 80 when he became the leader of Iran's Islamic government. He was born Ruhollah Moussavi and took his new name from his place of birth, the town of Khomein. 'Ayatollah' is the highest title a Shi'ite Muslim can hold, and it was given to Khomeini because of his skill in religious law and teaching. Ayatollah Khomeini died in 1989.

## After the revolution

Since the 1960s, one of the Shi'ite religious leaders, Ayatollah Khomeini, had been in exile. During the 1970s, Khomeini continued to speak out against the Shah, and most Iranians came to think of him as their true leader. He returned to Iran on 1 February 1979 to a huge welcome. Within a few weeks, Khomeini declared an Islamic republic. Iran was to be ruled according to the teachings of the Islamic holy book, the Koran. The new laws were harsh, and people who had worked for the Shah or who opposed the new government were executed.

On 22 September 1980 war broke out between Iran and Iraq. Today the effects of the war and the influence of the religious leaders is still affecting the lives of the Iranian people.

# Cory Aquino

On 21 August 1983, an aircraft landed at Manila airport in the Philippines. On board was a man called Benigno Aquino, who was coming home after three years abroad. As Aquino came down the aircraft steps, shots rang out and he fell dead on the runway.

Aquino was killed by supporters of Ferdinand Marcos, who had been president of the Philippines since 1965. When he first became president, Marcos used his power to help his people, the Filipinos, by building roads and schools and by improving farming methods. However, he soon began using his power to help his family and friends, and to protect his position as president. When elections were held, Marcos' supporters made sure that he received more votes than anyone else, so that he always won.

Benigno Aquino led a group of people who wanted fair elections, and he was put in prison by Marcos in the early 1970s. In 1980 Aquino was allowed to go to the United States for hospital treatment, and it was on his return that he was murdered.

Since the late 1960s, Marcos had also had problems with the Communists, who wanted land to be shared out among all Filipinos instead of being owned by just a few. Most Filipinos are Christians and, in some areas, Muslims wanted to set up independent governments. In 1972, as a result of the growing unrest, Marcos began using the army to keep law and order. He ended this in 1981, but it made even more Filipinos determined to free their country from Marcos' rule.

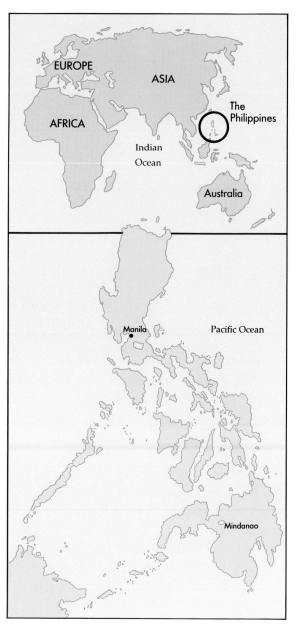

▲ People live on about a thousand of the 7000 islands that make up the Philippines. The country was part of the Spanish empire from 1565 to 1898, when it was taken over by the United States. It became a republic in 1946, with Manila as its capital.

## Cory Aquino takes over

After Benigno Aquino's murder, his wife, Cory, became leader of his group, which hoped that Marcos would lose the 1986 election. When the elections came, however, Marcos' supporters once again arranged for him to collect the most votes. Thousands of Cory Aquino's followers protested peacefully in the streets. Then most of the army joined Cory Aquino's side and Marcos had to leave the Philippines and go into exile. Cory Aquino became president of the Philippines.

The Philippines' problems were not over. Marcos' rule had left the country poor and difficult to govern. Marcos still had supporters among the people who had made money while he was president, and even today it is feared that they might try to overthrow the new government and bring Marcos back. The Communists also continue their protests, but most Filipinos hope that Cory Aquino's government will bring peace and wealth to their islands.

▲ Supporters of Cory Aquino waiting for her to arrive at Mindaneo during the presidential election campaign of 1986.

▼ Cory Aquino became president of the Philippines on 25 February 1986. She is seen here with Salvador Laurel who fought the election campaign with her and is now vice president.

# Time chart

| Date | Europe, Australia, New Zealand | Asia | Africa | North, Central and South America |
|------|-------------------------------|------|--------|----------------------------------|
| **AD** | | | | |
| 43 | Roman invasion of Britain | | | |
| 60 | Revolt of the Iceni against the Romans | | | |
| 1337 | Beginning of the Hundred Years War between Britain and France | | | |
| 1429 | Jeanne d'Arc's march to Orléans | | | |
| 1453 | End of the Hundred Years War. England loses all French possessions except Calais | | | |
| 1625 | Charles I becomes King of England | | | |
| 1642 | Start of the English Civil War Abel Tasman sights New Zealand | | | |
| 1644 | | Manchu family begins its rule of Chinese empire | | |
| 1648 | End of English Civil War | | | |
| 1649 | Execution of Charles I of England | | | |
| 1769 | Captain Cook lands in New Zealand | | | |
| 1770 | | | | The Boston Massacre |
| 1773 | | | | The Boston Tea Party |
| 1776 | | | | American Declaration of Independence |
| 1783 | | India Act gives Britain control of India | | End of the American War of Independence Birth of Simón Bolívar |
| 1789 | Start of the French Revolution | | | George Washington becomes first United States president |
| 1793 | Execution of Louis XVI of France | | | |
| 1833 | Garibaldi joins Young Italy | | | |
| 1840 | New Zealand becomes part of the British Empire on signature of the Treaty of Waitangi | | | |
| 1848 | The Year of Revolutions in Europe | | | |
| 1860 | Garibaldi and the Red Shirts capture Sicily Land Wars begin in New Zealand | | | |
| 1869 | | | Opening of Suez Canal | |
| 1870 | Italy united | | | |
| 1871 | End of the New Zealand Land Wars | | | |
| 1900 | | Boxer Rising in China | | |
| 1911 | | Chinese revolution | | |
| 1914 | | First World War begins | | |
| 1916 | Easter Uprising in Ireland | | | |

| Date | Europe, Australia, New Zealand | Asia | Africa | North, Central and South America |
|------|-------------------------------|------|--------|----------------------------------|
| 1917 | | The Russian Revolution begins and leads to civil war | | |
| 1918 | First World War ends | | | |
| 1920 | | Gandhi becomes leader of India National Congress | | |
| 1921 | Signing of the Anglo-Irish Treaty setting up the Irish Free State | | | |
| 1922 | | | Egypt becomes independent | |
| 1923 | | Mustafa Kemal Atatürk becomes president of Turkey | | |
| 1939 | Second World War begins | | | |
| 1941 | US enters Second World War | | | |
| 1945 | Second World War ends | | | |
| 1947 | | India gains independence from British rule | | |
| 1949 | Irish Free state becomes the Republic of Eire | Mao Tse-tung proclaims the People's Republic of China | | |
| 1952 | | | Free Officers' Revolution in Egypt The arrest of Jomo Kenyatta, after Mau Mau attacks begin in Kenya | |
| 1953 | | | Egypt becomes a republic | |
| 1956 | | | The Suez crisis | |
| 1959 | | | | The dictator Batista leaves Cuba, and Castro becomes leader of the government |
| 1961 | | | Jomo Kenyatta is freed from prison | |
| 1962 | | | | Cuban missile crisis |
| 1963 | | | Kenya becomes independent | |
| 1965 | | | | Ferdinand Marcos becomes president of the Philippines |
| 1971 | | East Pakistan becomes independent | | |
| 1979 | | Ayatollah Khomeini returns to Iran and declares an Islamic Republic | | |
| 1980 | | Shah of Iran dies in exile | | |
| 1983 | | | | Murder of Benigno Aquino |
| 1986 | | | | Ferdinand Marcos leaves the Philippines and Cory Aquino takes over the government |
| 1989 | | Death of Ayatollah Khomeini | | |

# Glossary

**allies:** a group of people or countries who have the same goals, and who come together to achieve them

**cavalry:** soldiers who fight on horseback

**Celtic:** a word used to describe the people who lived in Western Europe about 2500 years ago

**civil war:** a war between members of the same country, rather than between different countries

**colony:** a group of people who settle away from their own country, but still consider that they belong to it and are part of it

**Communist:** a person who believes in Communism, or that all members of a community should be equal. Communists believe that a country should be run by its workers, rather than by rulers

**conquer:** to take over by force

**corrupt:** to be dishonest, and not to be worthy of trust

**Dauphin:** the eldest son of the king of France. The dauphin will become king when his father dies

**democracy:** a country or part of a country where all the people have an equal say in who they want to govern them

**dictatorship:** a type of government where one person has complete power over everyone else in the country. Dictators usually have to use force to gain and keep their power

**election:** a way of choosing a government, or a leader. The people of a country vote for the political party, or person, whose ideas they agree with. The party with the most votes is elected and forms a government

**empire:** an area, or group of countries, which are all ruled by one country

**execute:** to kill someone as the punishment for a crime they have committed

**exile:** to live away from your own country, either by choice or as the result of being forced to leave

**explorer:** someone who travels to an area to find out more about it

**government:** a group of people who run, or govern, a city or country and make its laws

**guerrilla warfare:** fighting which is carried out by small, separate groups making surprise attacks on the enemy

**independent:** to be allowed to make decisions and to take action without having to ask permission from another person or country

**invade:** to enter somewhere without permission, usually by force

**missionary:** a religious worker who tries to spread his or her faith among non-believers

**moderate:** a person who has moderate political ideas and who believes that the way a country is run should be changed gradually

**nationalist:** a person who believes that the different areas of their country should stay together, and that the country should be governed by its own people

**parliament:** all the members of a government

**peasant:** a farm worker. Today we call them agricultural labourers

**plot:** to plan secretly

**policy:** a particular course of action, or change, which is taken by a government

**political party:** a group of people who share the same political ideas

**president:** the person elected by the people of a republic and who has overall power there

**Protestant:** a member of the part of the Christian Church which does not accept the Pope as its leader

**radical:** a person who has radical political ideas and who believes in making great changes in the running of a country, as quickly as possible

**rebellion:** an uprising of people who refuse to obey the government or the ruler of their country

**republic:** a country, or part of a country, which is ruled by its people through their chosen representatives

**reserve:** a place or piece of land which is set aside for a particular reason. For example, reserves are used to house people who have been removed from their homelands

**revolution:** a complete and sudden change in the way a country is governed when the people of that country overthrow their ruler or government

**riot:** a noisy and sometimes violent protest about something. A riot usually involves a crowd of people

**rule:** to have control over something. A country may be ruled by a government, or just by one person

**settler:** a person who leaves their homeland to settle, or live and work, in another place

**strike:** the action of a workforce refusing to work in protest against their employer

**tax:** a payment which the people of a country must make to their government. Taxes pay for the running of the government and all the services that it provides

**trader:** a person who earns their living by travelling the world buying and selling goods

**treaty:** a written agreement between people or countries who have disagreed with each other before

**union:** the coming together of a group of people, or countries, with the same ideas and goals

**unite:** to come together. People or countries are usually united by the same beliefs or by a need to achieve a particular goal

# Index